The
BLIZZARD
of
'78

On Cape Publications

Yarmouth Port, Massachusetts

Copyright © 2003

Edited by Stuard Derrick.

Production Supervisor Adam Gamble.

Graphic Design by DMAC.
E-mail: dmac@mts.net

ISBN 0-9719547-5-5

For more information please contact:

On Cape Publications
P.O. Box 218
Yarmouth Port, MA 02675
Toll free phone 1-877-662-5839
E-mail: Blizzardof78@oncapepublications.com

First Edition.
10 9 8 7 6 5 4

Printed in Canada.

Back Cover Photos. Left: Pulitzer Prize-winning photograph of Route 128, see page 26 for caption. Right: Former Coast Guard Beach bathhouse in Eastham from Cape Cod National Seashore, see page 36 for caption.

TABLE OF CONTENTS

To my mother, Jerri

ACKNOWLEDGEMENTS

I wish to thank the following people for sharing their photographs and for offering encouragement: Maureen Aldrich at *The Providence Journal*, Theodore Atkinson, Bauman Photography, The Boston Public Library, Lue Cheverie and Paul Scott at the Scituate Public Works Department, John Cronin and Kevin Cole at *The Boston Herald*, Dorothy Dudley, Alan Earls, Jim Gleason of *The Union-News*, Bob Gould, Allan Harris, Vin Horrigan, Len Kondratiuk at the Massachusetts National Guard Military Museum, John Koulbanis at *The Westerly Sun*, Gail Leach of the Bristol Historical Society, Dick Lucier, Tom Maguire, Hope Morrill at the National Park Service, Steve Mounior at the Springfield Library and Museum, Tom Neill, and Jane Nelson at *The Standard Times*.

I would also like to thank Stuard Derrick for his fine editing work and my publisher Adam Gamble whose creativity enhances each book we do together. ✳

CHAPTER 1

INTRODUCTION

INTRODUCTION

New Englanders were ill-prepared for the Blizzard of 1978. The day before the blizzard struck on February 5th, the Sunday edition of *The Boston Globe* called for snow that night, but there were no ominous references to a blizzard or severe storm. The forecast simply read, "Increasing cloudiness today, highs in the mid-20's. Tonight snow developing, low around 20. Monday, snow with high around 30."

Most residents of New England had already seen plenty of snow that year, and this forecast looked like a run-of-the-mill snowfall. Readers of *The Boston Globe* most likely focused on other news, such as the lead story regarding the latest Middle East peace initiative headlined, "Begin Responds to Sadat's Open Letter." Or they might have turned to the sports pages and read about the upcoming Beanpot hockey tournament, or glanced at a photo of Ernie DiGregorio with the caption, "Will the Celtics Give Him a Serious Shot?" Financially minded readers would have turned to the "Economy" section and learned that the Dow Jones Industrial Average had reached 770, but would most likely meet resistance when it approached 800.

On Monday morning, New Englanders awoke to cloudy skies but no falling snow. Some probably went straight to work, never giving the predicted snowfall a second thought. For those who had a chance to glance at the morning paper, there was nothing alarming to give them pause. Monday's *Boston Globe* called for snow ending on Tuesday. On the front page, in the upper "weather corner," there were no ominous warnings, but rather a whimsical caption, "You Sled It!" Inside the paper on the weather page, the prediction was for a "probable accumulation of six inches."

Commuters who had the time in the morning to listen to the radio or watch TV before leaving the house, might have learned that the snow would be heavy, and a major storm was on the way. The people of New England, however, had just experienced record snowfall two-and-a-half weeks earlier, and that storm did little damage. So the general population began their commute to work. After all, this was New England and snowfall is expected. ✳

▸
When the storm first hit Boston, pedestrians had as hard a time dealing with the wind as they did the snow. (photo: Angela Kaloventz/*The Boston Herald*)

◀ Cars lie buried under snow in downtown Providence. (photo: Richard Benjamin/*The Providence Journal*)

◀ Photographer Mark Murray caught this glimpse of the Springfield city skyline on Tuesday night. (photo: Mark Murray/*The Union-News*)

▲ Western Massachusetts and western Connecticut were able to dig out much faster than those areas to the east, but streets were still closed for two days. (photo: *The Union-News*)

▲ The Massachusetts National Guard used helicopters to bring critical supplies to snow-bound towns. (photo: Massachusetts National Guard Military Museum & Archives)

CHAPTER 2

THE STORM'S PROGRESSION & A COMMUTER'S NIGHTMARE

THE STORM'S PROGRESSION
&
A COMMUTER'S NIGHTMARE

The slight delay in the arrival of the snowflakes was a fateful turn of events, and most people went to work thinking the evening commute would be manageable. Some residents thought the storm had swung out to sea and would just brush New England. Still others guessed the snowfall would arrive later in the day, starting gradually as many storms do.

The first snowflakes arrived in the Boston/Providence area at roughly 10 a.m. Rather than starting off slow, the storm caught people off guard by hitting with almost full force. Snow accumulated quickly. Nervous office workers looked out windows during lunch and began to realize this was indeed a storm to be reckoned with. Those who had access to radios and TV would learn that the forecast for heavy snow had been upgraded to near blizzard conditions, and some had the foresight to head home immediately rather than wait for official office-closing announcements. By 1 p.m. snow was starting to drift on the streets, and winds were blowing up to forty miles an hour. Most offices began releasing workers beginning at 2 p.m., and the mass exodus was on. Commuters who traveled by bus, train and subway flocked to their respective stations, jamming the transit systems. Wind furiously whipped the snow, and conditions for pedestrians became unsafe as people walked with their backs to the wind or hunched over, trying to make progress as icy crystals stung exposed faces. Some pedestrians hung onto lightposts and street signs to keep from skidding into the street. Police formed lifelines along streets in Boston's Back Bay section to aid people across the roadways and prevent them from being blown into passing cars.

Conditions on the roadways were no better and were quickly becoming impassible. Front-wheel-drive and four-wheel-drive vehicles were not nearly as common as today. Spinning wheels could be heard on small hills, and vehicles slid sideways on the slightest curves. Disabled cars soon narrowed both side streets and major highways, and plows, already having difficulty keeping the blowing snow off roadways, were now impeded by the thousands of motorists who were desperately trying to get home.

Crossing bridges became a harrowing ordeal as winds increased to sixty miles an hour by mid-afternoon. Some motorists felt as if their cars would be swept right off the bridges. Trucks were especially vulnerable to the wind and ice, and jackknifed tractor-trailers caused havoc for commuters. One of the worst tractor-trailer accidents occurred on the Southeast Expressway at 3:30 p.m., when a truck skidded across the northbound lane into the southbound lane, blocking high-speed lanes on both sides.

From two to three p.m., traffic, if moving at all, was reduced to a crawl. By 4 p.m., almost every vehicle in greater Boston and Providence was stopped. Interstates 95 and 195 through Providence were wall-to-wall stalled cars and trucks, and Boston's Route 128 was clogged with 3,500 stranded vehicles, most of them stuck in the Needham to Canton stretch. States of emergency were declared, and the situation became desperate for many people trapped in cars or attempting to walk through whiteout conditions. The wind and the snarled traffic were actually more of a problem than the snow at that stage of the storm.

Some people waited in their cars for help, while others abandoned their vehicles, heading into the nearest towns or toward the nearest homes looking for shelter. Drivers who stayed in their cars later related their fears that the snow would cover their vehicles and they would never be found. Some recall their happiest moments were when they heard taps on their car roofs and looked out their windows to see the boots of state troopers. Incidents occurred where people suffered heart attacks or other medical emergencies and died because help was unable to reach them. In Providence, a makeshift morgue was set up in a cellblock for storm victims.

Shelters sprang up in places such as the Dedham Cinema where marooned motorists from Route 128 found warmth and food. Norwood Hospital, police stations and fire stations were also used as temporary shelters for snowbound commuters. Even the Boston Garden was put to use as a shelter for people who couldn't get home after the Beanpot Hockey Tournament. In Providence, where Interstate 95 goes through the city, people found their way to such shelters as the Civic Center and department stores. The two downtown Providence hotels, the Holiday Inn and the Marriott, were full, so people slept in the halls and corridors.

The most intense period of snowfall occurred in the early evening hours, with snow falling at a clip of three inches an hour. For those commuters still trapped in their cars, the night was lonely and terrifying, as they tried to keep warm while wondering if they would ever be found. People would stop and start their engines, trying to save fuel to power the heater. Most remembered to step outside and clear exhaust pipes every so often; each time this was done, drivers would become covered with snow, then return to their cars where the snow would melt, soaking their clothes in the cold darkness. Hypothermia became a very real danger. Stranded drivers on Providence's Interstate 195 felt a particular irony and frustration because they were surrounded by buildings, yet none could be reached. Motorists flashed their lights on and off in pleas for help.

Beginning on Monday night and into Tuesday, state troopers and National Guardsmen attempted to check every stuck car on the highways, and over 3,000 people were rescued in Rhode Island alone.

Sometimes a trooper or guardsman got there too late and discovered a frozen body, the victim of carbon monoxide poisoning.

Local citizens aided police in rescuing people from stranded cars. *The Walpole Times* reported that "snowmobilers saved the day," because by Monday night police cruisers were all stuck. Some snowmobilers rescued motorists unconscious from inhaling carbon monoxide fumes. *The Walpole Times* also noted that several stranded drivers did not reach safety until Tuesday night after spending Monday night and all day Tuesday trapped in their vehicles on Interstate 95. Some drivers like Kevin Rozak of Holyoke, Massachusetts, were stuck on Interstate 95 even longer. He later explained that he did not become nervous until Tuesday night when he awoke to find the cars around him evacuated. He crawled from the window of his automobile to get out and was picked up by a snowplow.

Not all travelers were stuck on the highways; some were lucky enough to make it to a hotel where they had to wait several days for the roads to clear. A typical stranding was reported by *The Springfield Republican* regarding a Longmeadow, Massachusetts, businessman who was trapped in Warwick, RI. "I was a prisoner of Rhode Island," said Irving Hirschfield. "It was an experience I hated to go through, but one I'll always remember. My wife warned me not to go, but I said you can't trust those weathermen." Hirschfield was able to get a hotel room, then watched as hundreds of others staggered in to sleep in the halls, lounges and restaurant. There was no heat Monday or Tuesday and limited food. Hirschfield passed the time by watching TV coverage of the storm to see when he could leave. He finally escaped the state on Friday by ignoring the travel ban. ✳

▸

Rhode Island's highways were just as bad as those in Massachusetts. Traffic on Interstate 95 through Providence came to a complete standstill. (photo: Robert Emerson/*The Providence Journal*)

▲ The intersection of Interstate 95 and 195 was one of the first places to grind to a halt, and commuters abandoned their vehicles. (photo: Andy Dickerman/*The Providence Journal*)

▲ These three pedestrians used a creative way to shelter themselves from the stinging snow. (photo: *The Boston Herald*)

▲ This Pulitzer Prize-winning photograph by Kevin Cole of *The Boston Herald* shows cars stranded in deep snow on Route 128. (photo: Kevin Cole/*The Boston Herald*)

▲ Although western Massachusetts received less snow than the eastern part of the state, commuters still experienced difficulties. (photo: *The Union-News*)

▲ A woman shields her face from stinging snow in New Bedford. (photo: *The Standard Times*)

▲ Although the New Bedford/Fall River area did not receive as much snow as Providence, cars were still abandoned in a haphazard fashion. (photo: *The Standard Times*)

▲ Two feet of snow and high winds made walking in Westerly, Rhode Island, a challenge. (photo: John Koulbanis/*The Westerly Sun*)

▲ Neither rain nor snow…. Although mail was suspended in most communities, postman
Bob Logan made his rounds in Westerly. (photo: John Koulbanis/*The Westerly Sun*)

▲ Route 1 in Norwood, Massachusetts, was no different than Route 128. (photo: Vin Horrigan)

▲ Some people waited in their cars while others abandoned their vehicles and walked to the nearest town for help. This scene is on Route 128 in Dedham. (photo: Vin Horrigan)

CHAPTER 3

THE COAST

THE COAST

On Monday evening when the new-moon high tide was at its crest, wind-driven waves thundered over seawalls, sweeping homes into the ocean, flooding coastal neighborhoods and stranding scores of frightened coastal dwellers. Seas crested at 16 feet above normal, turning homes blocks away from the shore into "ocean front" dwellings. Four consecutive high tides battered the coastline during the storm, accompanied by hurricane force winds reaching 79 miles per hour in Boston and 92 miles per hour in Chatham. (The coast of Massachusetts was hardest hit because the storm came out of the northeast, while Narragansett Bay protected Rhode Island's north-east facing shoreline.) Exposed areas were especially hard hit, including outer Cape Cod and the highly developed shorelines of Revere, Winthrop, Scituate, and Hull. Elderly people were especially vulnerable, and police, firemen, and good Samaritans launched rowboats to get to homes where people were trapped in waist-deep icy water.

Most of the storm's casualties occurred along the coast and on the ocean, such as the loss of a 5-man crew on a North Shore pilot boat, and a small rescue boat that capsized on the South Shore, drowning a young girl. The Gloucester pilot boat, the *Can Do*, was actually going to the aid of a tanker, the *Global Hope*, floundering just off Salem Sound; en route, the *Can Do* lost its navigation equipment in 30-foot waves and was never heard from again. Bodies of crewmembers from the pilot boat later washed up on North Shore beaches. The Coast Guard eventually used helicopters to evacuate the 32-man crew from the tanker.

Over 10,000 people were evacuated from exposed coastal areas, many taken away in small rescue boats. Piers were swept into the sea including Maine's Old Orchard Beach amusement pier, and Rockport's picturesque fishing shack referred to as Motif #1. In Boston, the *Peter Stuyvesant*, a ship turned into a cocktail lounge at Anthony's Pier 4 Restaurant on the waterfront, was capsized by the pounding waves.

Homes were not only clobbered by the enormous waves, but also by the debris hurled at them which included boulders, pebbles and mountains of sand. (An occasional lobster was also thrown on shore, providing a bonanza for those people who had a bottle of propane or a wood stove for cooking.) Roofs were blown off several homes while others were shaken from their foundations and ripped apart by the waves. Several homes were knocked from their foundations and pushed fifty feet inland by the surging surf. In Revere, lines were rigged to some houses to prevent them from being washed out to sea before the people trapped inside could be rescued. Front-end loaders were used to approach homes in flooded areas and carry out the residents in the giant scoops of the machines. In Nahant, a man drowned in his basement when he went to start the furnace.

In Eastham on Cape Cod, the dunes were obliterated along with the "Fo'castle," the cottage made famous by Henry Beston in his classic book, *The Outermost House*. Wallace Bailey, director of the Massachusetts Audubon Society at the time of the blizzard, described the demise of the Outermost House in two beautiful lines: "Strongly built and sturdy to the end, it quit its foundation posts and floated into the marsh. People watching through the fog from Fort Hill could see it, gable-deep but upright in the churning inland sea." (Knowing Beston's love and awe of the sea, the author himself might have thought the ocean, rather than old age, was a preferable ending for his beloved Fo'castle.) *

▶
Waves smash over Minot's light off the coast of Scituate. (photo: Kevin Cole/*The Boston Herald*)

◀ A view of the Coast Guard Beach parking lot in 1966. Note that the bathhouse in the rear of the photo rests on dunes several hundred feet from the ocean. (photo: Cape Cod National Seashore)

▶ Spectators in awe of the ocean's fury at the Coast Guard Beach parking lot during the storm. Compare this photograph to the preceding one. (photo: Cape Cod National Seashore)

◀ A boat has been swept from the ocean and deposited in front of the Scituate Playhouse on Cole Parkway. (photo: Town of Scituate)

◄ A furious surf battles with the dunes at Coast Guard Beach. (photo: Cape Cod National Seashore)

▲ After the storm receded, the extent of erosion on the Outer Cape became apparent. (photo: Cape Cod National Seashore)

▲ Even the access road to Coast Guard Beach was almost washed away. (photo: Cape Cod National Seashore)

◄ When the waves were finished with the parking lot, a good deal of it had been torn away. (photo: Cape Cod National Seashore)

41

▲ Henry Beston's cottage, "the Fo'Castle," was made famous in his book *The Outermost House* and became a National Literary Landmark. Prior to the blizzard it sat on the dunes of Nauset Marsh. (photo: Cape Cod National Seashore)

▲ Beston wrote of his beloved Fo'Castle, "Having known and loved this land for many years, it came about that I found myself free to visit there, and so I built myself a house upon the beach." Beston's cottage withstood many years of storms, but the Blizzard of '78 proved too much for the Fo'Castle. (photo: Cape Cod National Seashore)

▲ The blizzard swept the Fo'Castle from its perch. Beston loved watching a good storm and angry surf, writing, "Trampled by the wind and everlastingly moved and lifted up and flung down by the incoming seas, the water offshore becomes a furious glassiness of marbly foam; wild, rushing sheets of seethe fifty feet wide border it; the water streams with sand." (photo: Cape Cod National Seashore)

▲ The Fo'Castle is turned on its side and begins to sink. When Beston lived on the beach, he wrote of a tremendous winter storm, "A northeaster laden with sleet was bearing down on the Cape from off a furious ocean, an ebbing sea fought with a gale blowing directly on the coast: the lonely desolation of the beach was a thousand times more desolate in that white storm pouring down from a dark sky." (photo: Cape Cod National Seashore)

▲ The Manomet section of Plymouth, Massachusetts. The one-two punch of the January and February storms caused severe erosion and imperiled homes along the shoreline. (photo: Paul Benoit/*The Boston Herald*)

▲ Surging waves pounded this house into rubble in Kingston, Massachusetts. (photo: *The Boston Herald*)

◄ Two fishing boats have been pushed atop the broken pier in Scituate Harbor. (photo: Town of Scituate)

▲ The roof is still standing on this Brant Rock home in Marshfield, Massachusetts, but there is little supporting it. (photo: Vin Horrigan)

▲ Scituate's coast was hit so hard, the second stories of some homes were battered off the main structures. (photo: Theodore Atkinson)

▲ While snow blankets a section of Center Hill south of Nantasket Beach, sand and rubble dominated the beach front. Waves topped the breakwater, rendering it ineffectual. (photo: *The Boston Herald*)

◄ Trailers at Brant Rock in Marshfield, Massachusetts, were pushed around like flotsam. (photo: *The Boston Herald*)

▲ Plows had to push away debris rather than snow to clear Turner Road in Scituate. (photo: Town of Scituate)

◄ At Hampton Beach the only way to move was by boat. (photo: *The Boston Herald*)

▲ Instead of being stranded in three feet of snow, these two cars in Scituate are partially buried by three feet of rocks and pebbles coughed up by the ocean. (photo: Town of Scituate)

▲ It was heartbreaking for residents to return to their homes on the South Shore and find them completely destroyed. (photo: Kevin Cole/*The Boston Herald*)

▲ Surging waves did more damage to homes in Hull than the snow. Note the sand and rocks pushed into the house by the waves. (photo: Theodore Atkinson)

▲ Although Rhode Island's coast suffered less damage than Massachusetts, the home in the right of the photo (at Charlestown Beach, RI) was dragged on its concrete foundation closer to the waves. (photo: John Koulbanis/*The Westerly Sun*)

◄ In a joint effort by the U.S. Army Corps of Engineers and Civil Defense volunteers from Weymouth, Massachusetts, broken sections of shattered sea wall in the storm-lashed Nantasket Beach area are filled with sandbags in an effort to hold back the seas. (photo: *The Boston Herald*)

▲ Stanton Lane homes before the storm. (photo: Town of Scituate)

▲ Rebuilding on Stanton Lane. These homes are now elevated, but will this be enough to withstand the next great blizzard? (photo: Town of Scituate)

◄ Stanton Lane after the storm. All but one of the homes have been obliterated by the waves. Note that the home still standing appears to be missing its entire first floor shown in the prior photo. (photo: Town of Scituate)

▲ These homes at Hampton Beach, New Hampshire, were completely surrounded by water. (photo: *The Boston Herald*)

CHAPTER 4

SNOW REMOVAL

SNOW REMOVAL

In Rhode Island, government officials realized they did not have the necessary equipment to remove such incredible amounts of snow, and a request was made to the U.S. military for help. The plan was for the Air Force to fly huge cargo planes filled with heavy equipment into Rhode Island to help rescue people and clear paths for emergency equipment. But before this could be done, a landing strip at Green Airport in Providence needed to be cleared. Governor Garrahy of Rhode Island made clearing the airport of snow one of his top priorities. Plows were needed to clear a sixty-foot wide strip the entire length of one runway for the cargo planes to land. Drifting snow made the job extremely difficult: in some spots eight-foot drifts had formed and plows could only chip away at the snow, pushing two-foot sections from the drift's edge at each pass. Eventually 478 military troops were able to land, bringing 178 pieces of equipment.

The heavy equipment was immediately put to work to open Interstates 95 and 195. State crews cleared a one-lane path primarily in the center lane that not only served as an emergency lane but also allowed wreckers to move abandoned vehicles into this cleared area. The larger plows and front-end loaders then moved snow off the outside lanes, and by Thursday night much of the highway had been cleared except for stalled cars packed in the center lane. On Friday, drivers searched for their cars, and much of the traffic jam began to disappear. (Governor Garrahy also hired over one-hundred drivers and heavy plows from Buffalo, New York to augment the federal troops and Rhode Island's equipment.)

While conditions were improving on the highways, Providence itself was still a mess. Snow removal efforts were so difficult in the snow-clogged streets that Mayor Buddy Cianci not only imposed a ban on vehicles, but also on all pedestrians because they were impeding plows. Progress was made on the Friday and Saturday after the blizzard, but even as late as Sunday and early Monday, one week after the storm, the city was still closed to traffic. Many Providence businesses did open, but workers had to take special buses from out-lying areas into the city. The traffic ban was finally lifted late Monday morning.

In greater Boston, the situation was equally serious. Governor Michael Dukakis had called out the National Guard and Army troops from Fort Devens, and they were later joined by 1,000 Federal troops flown into Logan Airport on Wednesday evening. Unclogging the mess on Route 128 was a piecemeal effort. Guards-men, Army troops, and highway crews used front-end loaders to scoop up enough snow around each car to allow its removal by a tow truck. After several cars had been removed, a plow would then clean that area. Teams of plows, wreckers and front-end loaders worked from both the north and south. To clear just a half-mile took approxi-mately four hours. (The blizzard came just two-and-a-half weeks after another heavy snowfall. In some areas the snowbanks from the preceding storm made it even more difficult to move and dump the newly accumulated snow.) ❋

▲ This southbound view of Route 128 has the message "Snow Bound" written in the snow in the foreground. (photo: Vin Horrigan)

▲ Progress was measured car by car. (photo: Vin Horrigan)

◄ Front-end loaders were used to dig out stranded vehicles and provide access for tow trucks. It was a very slow process. (photo: Vin Horrigan)

▲ Troops and snow fighting equipment are unloaded from the mouth of a giant Air Force C-5-A transport which arrived at Logan Airport on Friday, February 10. (photo: Bob Howard/*The Boston Herald*)

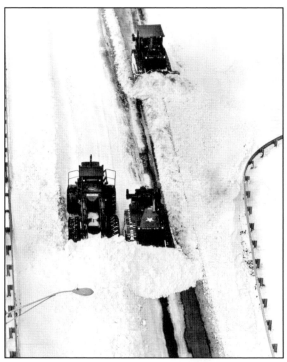

◀
Army plows clear Route 295 in Warwick. The plows had to make several passes over the same stretch of highway. (photo: *The Providence Journal*)

▶
The Massachusetts section of Interstate 195 is clear to the state line, while the Rhode Island section remains snow-covered. (photo: Andrew Dickermans/ *The Providence Journal*)

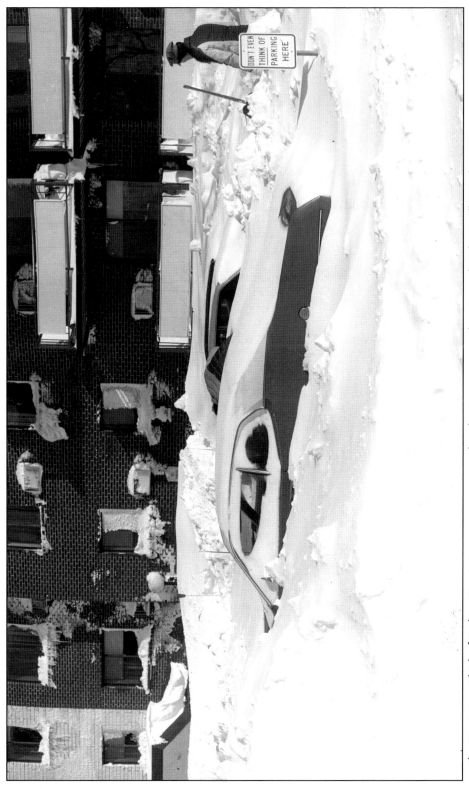

◀ The 'Don't Even Think of Parking Here' sign was unnecessary, but digging out was a daunting task. (photo: Allen Joel Harris)

▲ Shoveling was a back-breaking effort, but most homeowners had little choice. (photo: *The Union-News*)

▲ Military equipment helps clear a narrow path on Falmouth Street in Attleboro. (photo: Tom Maguire)

▲ This photograph shows why it was almost impossible for plows to clear Attleboro's streets. Front-end loaders were more effective because they could lift the snow over the growing snow banks. (photo: Tom Maguire)

▲ Work goes quicker when there are many hands … and strong backs on North Main Street, Attleboro. (photo: Tom Maguire)

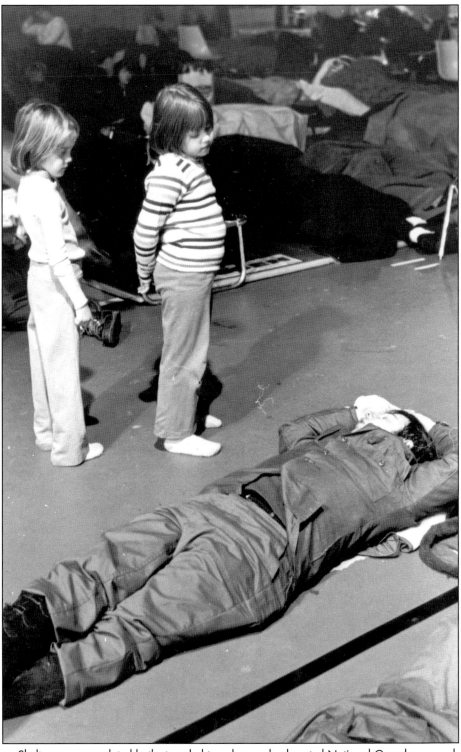

▲ Shelters accommodated both stranded travelers and exhausted National Guardsmen and Army troops. (photo: Paul Benoit/*The Boston Herald*)

▶ The team approach to snow removal. (photo: *The Union-News*)

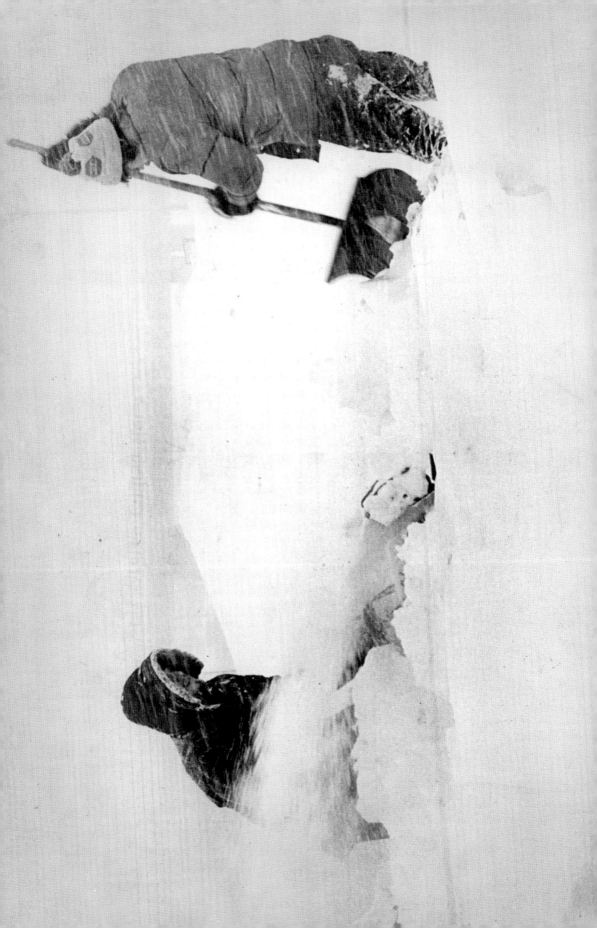

◀ Smaller plows had to get a running start, then ram into the snow to move small sections at a time. (photo: *The Standard Times*)

◄ It took eight hours of work to shovel a single passage to this car. (photo: Bob Gould/Dick Lucier)

▲ The Massachusetts National Guard used their heavy equipment to clear streets that were covered with sand washed up from the ocean. (photo: Massachusetts National Guard Military Museum & Archives)

CHAPTER 5

DESTRUCTION
& CASUALTIES

DESTRUCTION & CASUALTIES

Fifty-four people in Massachusetts and twenty-one people in Rhode Island lost their lives as a result of the storm. Some died from drowning in the ocean, others from heart attacks from shoveling or slogging through the snow, and a few from carbon monoxide poisoning due to snow-clogged automobile tailpipes. Car accidents and prolonged exposure to the cold also claimed victims. Freak accidents occurred as well, such as electrocution due to individuals stepping on fallen wires buried beneath the snow.

Medical emergencies were handled by snowmobiles, four-wheel-drive trucks and National Guard helicopters. These same helicopters were also used to ferry food to delivery points, where it would then be distributed to stores and restaurants. The storm revealed just how dependent New England was on trucking as its main means of transporting essential goods.

Hundreds of houses were destroyed, and almost 6,000 residences were damaged. A handful of homes were consumed by fire because firemen simply couldn't get to the scene to fight the blaze. In Minot Beach, on Massachusett's South Shore, one home was destroyed when it caught fire due to floodwaters short-circuiting its electrical wiring; this same water prevented fire apparatus from reaching the home. Total monetary damage from the storm was estimated at over a billion dollars.

Although largely forgotten, looting did occur during the storm when thieves took advantage of the abandoned stores. In the first three days of the storm, 125 people were arrested in Boston, most of them on Tuesday night. Exhausted police officers were helped by National Guardsmen in beefing up the police presence in troubled areas. Abandoned cars were also broken into and there were cases of price gouging.

To alleviate the suffering of those whose home heating oil had run out, the state of Rhode Island established emergency pick-up points, where families were allowed to take up to forty gallons of oil in their own containers. Over 2,000 people took advantage of the offer, hauling away oil in jugs, plastic tubs, and gas cans. *

▲ In Boston, snow removal was hampered by stranded cars – some even on the sidewalks. Hundreds of cars were damaged in accidents. (photo: The Boston Public Library)

▲ Besides the destruction from snow and wind, there was also the threat of fires that could not be controlled. (photo: *The Union-News*)

▲ At Anthony's Pier 4 in Boston, the *SS Stuyvesant*, which was used as a cocktail lounge, sank. (photo: Vin Horrigan)

▲ The wind and waves did more damage than the snow along the coast of Massachusetts. (photo: *The Boston Herald*)

▶ This milkman still made his rounds even though his truck wasn't going anywhere. (photo: *The Boston Herald*)

▲ The National Guard used helicopters to bring in desperately needed medical supplies.
(photo: *The Boston Herald*)

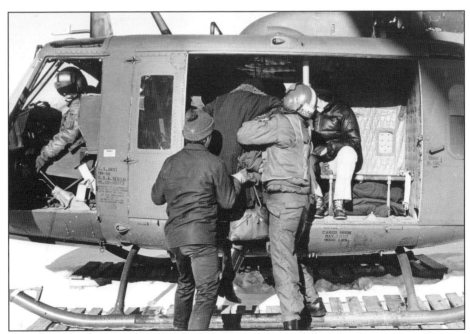

▲ Helicopters were also used to evacuate stranded people who needed medical attention.
(photo: *The Boston Herald*)

◀ Towns north of Boston such as Winthrop, Revere, Lynn and Nahant incurred serious damage along their shore-fronts. (photo: Massachusetts National Guard Military Museum & Archives)

▲ Without snowmobiles to rescue stranded motorists, there would have been many more casualties. (photo: Massachusetts National Guard Military Museum & Archives)

▲ Even the Massachusetts National Guard medical trucks sometimes needed a push. (photo: Massachusetts National Guard Military Museum & Archives)

CHAPTER 6

AFTER THE STORM

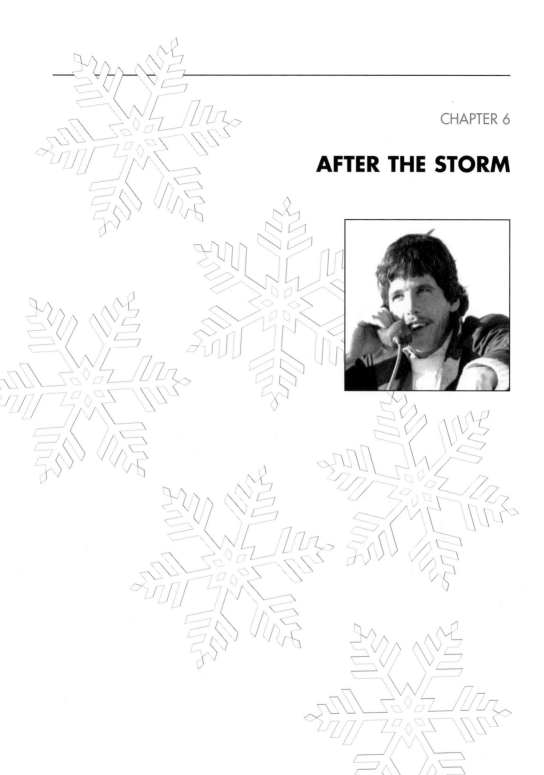

AFTER THE STORM

In addition to the expected problems of electrical outages, and food shortages due to transportation disruptions, there were other problems such as the fact that Boston experienced a money shortage. As reported by *The Associated Press*, "Thousands wandered snowy streets in search of banks that might be open and stores that had supplies. They climbed over snow that in spots was plowed as high as traffic lights. 'There's no money. The banks can't get their people in to open up,' said Michael Wartell, manager of a branch of Blanchard's liquor supermarket. 'People beg us to cash checks.'" Some banks did open but established a maximum withdrawal of $100 per person.

To allow snowplows and front-end loaders to remove snow from streets, driving was not allowed for several days after the storm. Instead, people walked, snowshoed and skied, pulling their groceries on sleds. They took time to stop and chat with strangers, exchanging stories, giving advice, and sharing a laugh. Neighbors shoveled out neighbors and purchased groceries for those unable to do so themselves. Many snowbound people had no electricity for days, and battery-powered radios were their link with the outside world. Besides listening to storm updates, they could entertain themselves with the latest hit songs from *Saturday Night Fever*.

Neighbors suffering from cabin fever tried all sorts of remedies: some set up card tables in the snow and served wine and cheese, others had neighborhood cookouts using their gas and charcoal grills.

For those who were stranded in their cars it was a nerve-wracking experience, and in some cases life-threatening; but many experienced the best side of human compassion. Total strangers opened their doors to marooned motorists and shared what they had. Many became life-long friends.

Recollections of the aftermath of the blizzard usually tend to be fond memories of neighborhoods rallying together to help one another, and the spirit of camaraderie of people who were battered and bruised by a common foe and survived. One friend recalled the days after the storm as follows: "It's almost as if the people in your neighborhood all got transported through space to a new, wondrous place – a place similar to old surroundings but in place of rough square edges and straight lines were white curves. A place where cars are not allowed and people cannot hurry." Others recalled the days after the blizzard as "a chance to slow down and reconnect with family and friends. We walked to the store, went sledding and played games by the fireplace. Without electricity we cooked on the fire or outside on the grill. It was fun."

The Walpole Times reported that the most frequently heard comment was, "The town should do something like this once a month: ban cars on every thoroughfare and give them back to foot traffic." *The Times* went on to report, "There was an oddly buoyant mood to the town and a near carnival air as people, pedestrians, had their town to themselves for the first time in years."

On a prior book project this writer interviewed many people who lived through the Hurricane of 1938, and the instant recollection of distant memories was surprising. I suspect those who experienced the Blizzard of '78 will remember every detail even at the 50th Anniversary of the event. People will never forget their adventures during the Blizzard of '78. ✳

▸

People remarked how pleasant it was not to have cars on the road. Strangers would stop and talk, sharing blizzard stories. (photo: The Boston Public Library)

▲ Boston streets were closed to vehicles for a week, and the only means of travel was on foot, or by sleds, cross-country skis or snowshoes. (photo: The Boston Public Library)

◀ It will be a long time before cross-country skiers and walkers can again travel down the middle of Route 128. (photo: Vin Horrigan)

▲ Cabin fever made folks a little impatient to have their streets plowed. Some side streets were not plowed for a week. (photo: *The Standard Times*)

▲ "A Conversation Piece".… (photo: S. Bauman)

▲ Two days after the storm, this Providence man was lucky enough to get milk and bread after waiting in line. (photo: Robert Emerson/*The Providence Journal*)

▲ These two daring individuals take a leap off the East Street Bridge over Route 128. (photo: Vin Horrigan)

⏶ One week after the storm, people came back to the city to work; but the roads were closed to all vehicles except for public transportation. (photo: *The Boston Herald*)

⏶ A long line of shoppers waiting for the Stop and Shop in Revere to open. (photo: Angela Kaloventzos/*The Boston Herald*)

▲ Skiers ruled the roads in Attleboro. (photo: Tom Maguire)

▲ Boston Mayor Kevin White thanks the Massachusetts National Guard for their service. (photo: Massachusetts National Guard Military Museum & Archives)

▲ Neighbors band together to do what the plows did not do. (photo: *The Standard Times*)

CHAPTER 7

SNOWFALL TOTALS

SNOWFALL TOTALS

Although wind and tides created the majority of the damage along the coast, the tremendous amount of snowfall crippled inland communities for a week. While Cape Cod snowfall was mixed with rain, and snow accumulation was under a foot, just fifty miles inland towns along the Massachusetts/Rhode Island border such as Woonsocket, Rhode Island, had 38 inches of snow.

According to the National Weather Service, the Blizzard of '78 was the worst storm to hit southern New England in the 20th century. It also broke the record for the single largest storm to ever hit Massachusetts. The Blizzard of '78 came on the heels of another backbreaking storm that had hit the region just 18 days earlier. That storm had almost as much snow, but the blizzard that slammed into New England on February 6th had hurricane-force winds that whipped the drifts higher and swelled the tides larger. *The Boston Globe* reported that "Boston snowfall in the 24-hour period that ended at 7 p.m. yesterday [February 7th] totaled 23.6 inches, a record. The prior record of 21.4 inches was set in the last storm only 18 days ago."

Regional snowfall totals for the Blizzard of 1978 in Rhode Island and Massachusetts were as follows:
- Massachusetts North Shore: 24 to 30 inches.
- Boston: 27 inches.
- Western Massachusetts: 12 to 24 inches.
- Central Massachusetts: 24 to 30 inches.
- Southeastern Coastal Massachusetts: 12 to 24 inches.
- Rhode Island and the Massachusetts area near the southern half of Route 495: 30 to 38 inches.

The heaviest snowfall fell in a circular area that stretched through most of Rhode Island into a region of Massachusetts roughly bounded by Massachusetts Turnpike to the north, Route 24 to the east, and westward into the Blackstone Valley. Officially, this area received 30 to 38 inches of snow but several towns unofficially reported a snowfall of 50 inches.

Other states:

- Eastern Connecticut: 24 to 30 inches. (Governor Ella Grasso declared a State of Emergency and asked President Carter to declare the state a Federal Disaster Area. Damage was in excess of 25 million dollars, over 5,000 people fled to emergency shelters, and there were three deaths.)
- Southern Maine and New Hampshire: 12 to 24 inches, with some serious coastal flooding.
- Vermont: two to three feet of snow fell in some sections of Southern Vermont, no deaths.
- New York City: 18-21 inches, at least two dead.
- New Jersey: 18 inches fell, with snowdrifts up to nine feet on rural roads. At least seven dead.
- Pennsylvania: more than two feet fell on parts of Eastern Pennsylvania, at least four dead.

(The oddest tidbit I came across in my research is that according to *The Union-News* the storm actually had a name — "Larry". And the best snow related quote I've come across was from Mae West who said, "I used to be Snow White, but I drifted.")

▸

After a morning of aiding stranded motorists, Kevin Gouvin of Westerly, Massachusetts, has time for fun, giving Dave Palmer a ride on his "Flying Saucer." (photo: John Koulbanis/*The Westerly Sun*)

**TOTAL SNOWFALL
(IN INCHES)
BLIZZARD OF 1888**

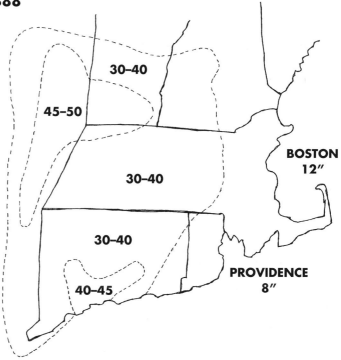

30–40

45–50

BOSTON
12"

30–40

30–40

PROVIDENCE
8"

40–45

**TOTAL SNOWFALL
(IN INCHES)
BLIZZARD OF 1978**

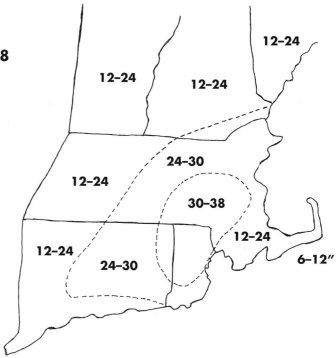

12–24

12–24

12–24

12–24

24–30

12–24

30–38

12–24

12–24

24–30

6–12"

◄ Drifts reach the windows of mobile homes in Taunton, where snowfall exceeded three feet. (photo: Dorothy Dudley)

FORMATION OF THE BLIZZARD

The storm occurred when cold upper-level air pushed down from the Great Lakes during Saturday night, February 4th, and headed southeastward. When it hit the ocean, the warm water and high humidity created a low-pressure system. On Sunday night, the storm was southeast of North Carolina's Cape Hatteras and began to move northward following the prevailing wind up the coast. As it traveled northward it fed on the warm water below and cold air from the north, growing into a monster storm. Meteorologists reported that as the storm reached New England it stalled because a "vertical stack" occurred, with an upper-level low on top and a surface low beneath. The warm, wet air rose over the cold and then froze as it fell through the cold layer to the ground. Satellite photos from the period show tight spiral clouds, similar to a hurricane, swirling just south of Cape Cod. ✽

EXAMINING THE TERM "BLIZZARD"

England, Germany and America lay claim to the term "blizzard." The English believe it comes from a common expression, "May I be blizzered!". Germany states its origin derives from "Blitz," meaning lightning. Another theory is that Americans used the term "blizzer" to describe a cannon shot, or a flash, and altered the word to describe a storm. The first use of the word to describe a snowstorm may have been by an Iowa newspaper in the 1870's. The U.S. Weather Bureau defines a blizzard as a snowstorm with winds of at least 35 mph and temperatures 20 degrees Fahrenheit or lower. ✽

OTHER NEW ENGLAND BLIZZARDS
& CRUEL WINTERS

The Winter of 1716–17

Snow fell almost continuously in January and February of 1717, making travel next to impossible and isolating rural homes for months. "People were overwhelmed with snow," wrote Cotton Mather. "The odd accidents befalling many poor people whose cottages were totally covered with snow, and not the very tops of the chimneys to be seen, would afford a story." Even the Native Americans still living in New England said their fathers never mentioned a prior winter as bad as this one. Deer were driven from the forests by starvation and into coastal areas in search of food. (So many deer perished that officers, called deer-reeves, were elected by various towns to protect the few deer that managed to survive.) Cattle and sheep were smothered in snow and some were found frozen weeks later, still standing where they had died. Some sheep entombed in great drifts survived by eating the wool off the dead sheep around them. Tunnels were dug from house to barn. After the storm, it took a postman nine days on snowshoes to travel the forty miles from Salem, Massachusetts to Portsmouth, New Hampshire.

The Winter of 1740–41

Extreme cold froze the harbors of Boston and New York, blocking incoming ships with provisions and freezing in place those already in the harbors. Water that powered mills froze to the bottom of ponds, preventing corn from being ground. Even as late as May there were still traces of snow around Boston.

The Winter of 1786–87

A series of December storms lashed all of New England with snow, wind and ocean swells. Two men from Rowley, Massachusetts, were clamming when the storm hit and soon became lost in the blinding snow. Growing desperate and weak, they burrowed into a stack of salt hay to wait out the storm. They passed the night there and when morning came, the tide had risen so high that they had to climb to the top of the stack to stay out of the water. When a cake of ice slammed into the haystack, it became dislodged and the men were driven around the marsh by the wind. As the stack began to break apart, they got lucky when a second stack of hay floated by and they leapt to that one. They were pushed four miles northward through the marshes before the wind shifted and began to blow them toward the open ocean. At this point they decided to risk leaving the protection of the haystack and leapt onto an ice flow that they managed to paddle to the shore and eventual safety.

The Winter of 1801–02

A blizzard struck the New England coast in February, during a period when schooners plied the waters off Cape Cod. The *Brutus*, a full-rigged sailing ship, floundered off Truro and the sailors lightened the ship by jettisoning cargo. Then the ship was blown closer to shore where it became stuck on a sandbar. The masts were immediately cut, but the ship started to break apart. The main mast had fallen toward the beach side, and sailors attempted to crawl on it to get closer to land. Some were swept away and drowned, but others made it to shore. They beached in an isolated region, however, and had to trudge through the darkness of a bitterly cold night to find safety. As they staggered in the direction of Provincetown, one by one members of the party were overcome with fatigue, lay down in the snow, and died. Five men eventually made it to a lighthouse where they found help and survived. ❋

CHAPTER 8

COMPARING THE BLIZZARD OF 1888 TO THE BLIZZARD OF 1978

COMPARING THE BLIZZARD OF 1888
TO THE BLIZZARD OF 1978

The Blizzard of 1888 damaged a larger area than the Blizzard of 1978 and is known as the worst blizzard to occur in the last 200 years. The Blizzard of 1888 hit during the evening of March 11th, and its fury extended from Washington, D.C. northward to Maine, and from New York westward to Pittsburgh. Sections of Connecticut and Massachusetts were especially hard hit, with 40 to 50 inches of snow falling and drifts up to 40 feet.

The death toll exceeded 400, 300 of which occurred on land and the remaining 100 at sea. Two-hundred ships were sunk or damaged. Many of the casualties could be attributed to lack of accurate weather forecasting at the time. In fact, forecasters often took Sundays off, which happened to be the day the blizzard hit. The Sunday edition of *The New York Herald* did not even call for snow: "In this city and suburban districts today colder, partly cloudy to fair weather and brisk to fresh westerly to northwesterly winds will probably prevail followed by clear conditions." (Weather forecasting improved when instruments could be carried aloft by weather balloons in the 1890's, allowing high-altitude observations.)

Unlike the Blizzard of 1978, the Blizzard of 1888 hit western Massachusetts harder than eastern Massachusetts. Although the storm was centered off Long Island, its front cut a north-south swath through the center of New England. Warm air was to the east of the front, and coastal areas received mostly sleet and rain. West of the line, however, temperatures were extremely cold, hovering just above zero degrees Fahrenheit. While Boston only got 12 inches of snow, Worcester, just 45 miles to the west, received 32 inches. Providence and Block Island received only eight inches and six inches of snow respectively, but New Haven, Connecticut, located to the southwest, had 45 inches.

Thirty-five to fifty inches of snow blanketed central and western Massachusetts, and almost all of Connecticut, southern Vermont, the Hudson River Valley of New York and southwestern New Hampshire. Drifts reached an astounding height of forty feet, totally covering many homes. Bitter temperatures were also drawn from the north, and pushed southward into New York, New Jersey and Pennsylvania, which received heavy snowfall as well.

The Blizzard of 1978 might have been just as devastating as the one in 1888 had we not had helicopters, snowplows, snowmobiles and other modern emergency equipment. Back in 1888, snow removal was by manual labor using horse and oxen, and communication systems were primitive by our standards. The transportation used for lengthy travel in 1888 was either by train or ship, and both were completely shut down by snow, wind and waves. Hundreds of people were stranded in trains that became stuck on the tracks. One such incident involved the plight of 95 people marooned in Saybrook, Connecticut, aboard the Shore Line Express that ran from Boston to New York. The conductor attempted to walk one mile to the nearest station, but barely made it in the blinding snow, crawling the last few yards. (His ears were frozen, and at the time the treatment for frostbite was to rub and pack the affected areas with snow, which we now know only made things worse.) He later recovered enough to return back to the train and inform the passengers that they should prepare to spend the night, or perhaps two, as no assistance was forthcoming. Sanitation on board worsened by the hour and food was in short supply. There were only a few crackers on the train, but passengers helped themselves to the ample liquor that was available. In the morning, a few men struck out for a farmhouse and returned with food. Soon, local people arrived at the train, bringing more provisions and taking passengers home with them.

On another train stuck in Shelburne, Vermont, passengers broke into the sealed express car and found tenderloin steaks bound for Boston, which they cooked on frying pans improvised from coal shovels. Not everyone who suffered through the blizzard was so lucky. On the New York and Harlem Railroad, locomotives tried to crash through towering drifts. The newspapers described what happened next: "Rushing into the mounds at a rate of forty miles and hour, four men were instantly killed."

Hartford, Connecticut, and Springfield, Massachusetts, were clobbered with 36 inches of snow. Some workers did go to work Monday, March 12, despite the raging snowstorm, because they were afraid they would lose their jobs if they missed a day's work. When it was time to return home, pedestrians found the city streets that were normally lit by the soft glow of gas lights or the newer electric lights were in total darkness.

The disruption of food supplies to city dwellers was especially critical because at the time people shopped daily for products that lasted only for the next twenty-four hours. (Refrigerators were not available and old wooden iceboxes were commonly used, so urban residents usually depended on fresh meat, produce and dairy from local markets on a daily basis.) The blizzard prevented new supplies from getting through, and what provisions were left in the market were often priced at astronomical levels.

Fuel distribution, especially coal, came to a halt, and those city dwellers whose coal bins were empty huddled in freezing apartments and homes. In New York, housewives wandered the city with tin pails, hoping to find a store that still had coal. Police were called to one grocery store where women had converged in front of the coal bins, demanding coal they thought the owners were hoarding.

Conditions in the countryside were no better. In some areas people were stranded for two weeks, and those who did try to move about found they were walking over treetops! Twelve storm refugees trapped in a house near Hartford became so desperate for food they gathered up the frozen sparrows lying near the dooryard and made a pie out of them.

Because the Blizzard of 1888 claimed more lives and covered a broader region than the Blizzard of 1978, it gets top billing as the worst blizzard on record to ever hit the eastern United States. In greater Providence and Boston, however, there is no comparison: the Blizzard of 1978 is still the granddaddy of all winter storms. *

▶
Trolley cars became stuck in the snow in Springfield, Massachusetts, and horses proved more reliable in 1888. (photo: The Springfield Public Library)

◀ The Blizzard of 1888 hit interior Massachusetts harder than its coast. On Main Street in Springfield, the paths for pedestrians and horse drawn carriages were separated by huge banks of snow. (photo: The Springfield Public Library)

◄ Snow accumulated on the section of tracks running through a rock cut and buried this locomotive. Some passengers were trapped on trains for three days. (photo: Bristol Historical Society)

◄ At the Emmett Street Crossing in Bristol, this train became stuck. (photo: Bristol Historical Society)

◄ This photograph at the Emmett Street Crossing shows the depth of the snow drifts. (photo: Bristol Historical Society)

◂ In addition to stalled trains, railroad stations were also snowed-in. (photo: Bristol Historical Society)

◂ At Bristol's News Depot, these serious looking men and boys are dwarfed by the snowbanks on the street. (photo: Bristol Historical Society)

▲ Looking down Main Street in Bristol, Connecticut. Note that the snow has been shoveled off the sidewalks and into the street. (photo: Bristol Historical Society)

◀ In 1888, snow had to be shoveled onto horse-drawn sleighs and hauled off the streets. (photo: The Connecticut Historical Society, Hartford, Connecticut)

About the Author

Michael Tougias is the author of several books about New England and gives frequent slide presentations, including one about the Blizzard of 1978. He is interested in reviewing more unique blizzard photos for future editions. Please send a photocopy of your best images to: M. Tougias, P.O. Box 72, Norfolk, MA 02056. Those interested in having him speak or present a slide show may also write to this address.

Ordering Books

To order autographed copies of Tougias' books send a check to the author at PO Box 72, Norfolk, MA 02056 and include $2.00 for shipping. His books are as follows:

- *Quabbin: A History and Explorers Guide* ($18.95)
- *There's a Porcupine in My Outhouse!* ($18.95)
- *River Days: Exploring the Connecticut River from Source to Sea* ($14.95)
- *King Philip's War: The History and Legacy of America's Forgotten Conflict* (co-author Eric Schultz) ($18.95)
- *Until I Have No Country* (A novel of King Philip's War) ($14.95)
- *New England Wild Places* ($12.95)
- *Autumn Rambles of New England* (co-author Mark Tougias) ($14.95)
- *Quiet Places of Massachusetts* ($13.95)
- *Nature Walks in Eastern Massachusetts* ($12.95)
- *More Nature Walks in Eastern Massachusetts* ($12.95)
- *Nature Walks in Central and Western Massachusetts* (co-author R. Laubach) ($12.95)
- *Country Roads of Massachusetts* ($13.95)
- *Exploring the Hidden Charles* ($12.95)
- *A Taunton River Journey* ($10.95)

YOUR BLIZZARD RECOLLECTIONS*

*If you would like to have your recollections of the Blizzard of '78 considered for future publications of this book, please email to yourblizzardrecollections@oncapepublications.com.

127